Award Winning Secret BBQ Recipes

by

C. Anthony Howe

Contents

CHICKEN
    Maple Barbecued Chicken
    Barbecued Orange Chicken
    Grilled Key Lime Chicken
    Garlic Chicken
    Chicken Marinade

BEEF
    Beef Sauces
    Barbecued Chuck Roast
    Bourbon Steak
    Tangy Rib Eye Steaks
    Marinated Steak Kabobs

PORK
    Grilled Pork Shoulder Steaks

FISH
    Grilled Halibut With Oriental Sauce

RIBS
    Memphis-Style Barbecued Ribs
    Baby Back Ribs With Mustard Sauce
    Oven BBQ Ribs
    Pineapple Baby Back Ribs
    Apple Smoked Barbecue Ribs
    Kansas City Rib Rub

WINGS
    Cinnamon Honey Wings

SHRIMP
Shrimp On The Barbie.
MISC SAUSES & RUBS
Beer Barbecue Sauce
Honey Spiced BBQ Sauce
Jack Daniel's Grilling Sauce
Watermelon Barbecue Sauce
Tennessee BBQ Sauce
Molasses Orange Barbecue Sauce
Carolina BBQ Rub
Cajun Blackening Spices

Grill Masters CHICKEN

Chicken Sauces

If you're looking to spice up another ho-hum chicken dinner then nothing better than barbecue sauce.

The **grill masters** have assembled their top five award winning recipes that are sure to have you been looking at chicken quite the same way ever again!

Maple Barbecued Chicken

4 Skinless Chicken Thighs
1 Tablespoon of Cider Vinegar
1 Tablespoon of Canola Oil
3 Tablespoons of Maple Syrup
2 Teaspoon of Dijon Mustard
3 Tablespoons of Chili Sauce

Preheat your grill.

Combine vinegar, syrup, chili sauce, & mustard
together in a saucepan.

Let everything simmer for 5 minutes.

Brush the chicken with your canola oil, then season
with salt and pepper.

Place your chicken on the grill and cook for 10 to 15
minutes or until fork tender.

Remember to occasionally turn & generously brush
with the sauce during the last few minutes of grilling.

Barbecued Orange Chicken

2 1/2 Pounds of Assorted Chicken

BBQ Sauce:
1/4 Cup of Tomato Paste
1/4 Cup of Frozen Orange Juice Concentrate
1/4 Cup of Vegetable Oil
1/2 Cup of White Wine Vinegar
1 Orange Zest (removed with grater)

Salad:
1 Orange, Sectioned (Without Rind)
1 Large, Ripe Tomato
1 Tablespoon of White Wine Vinegar
1 Tablespoon of Vegetable Oil
2 Scallions, Chopped
1/8 Teaspoon of Pepper
1/8 Teaspoon of Salt

Prepare your grill & begin heating your coals.

Take a medium sized bowl & mix together the barbecue ingredients until evenly smooth.

Place the chicken skin-side-down on your grill away from the center of the heat.

Let it cook for about 15 minutes.

Turn chicken over & continue grilling for an additional 10 minutes.

Brush the chicken with your BBQ sauce & occasionally turn over the chicken for an additional 10 minutes until thoroughly cooked.

Slice the tomato into wedges & place into a different medium sized bowl.

Using a paring knife, cut out the white pith off the orange.

Remove orange colored sections & add them to tomato slices.

Sprinkle the salad with your oil, scallions, & vinegar.

Toss the salad to mix everything up & continue by seasoning it with salt and pepper.

Toss again & serve with the chicken.

Grilled Key Lime Chicken

3 Pounds of Boneless Skinless Chicken Breasts
3/4 Cup of Water
1 Tablespoon of Honey
1 Cup of Key Lime Juice
2 Tablespoons of Vegetable Oil
1/2 Teaspoon of Ground Thyme
1 Tablespoon of Fresh Ginger, Peel, Grated
1/2 Teaspoon of Fresh Ground Black Pepper

Mix all listed ingredients (except chicken) with a blender or food processor.

Process until smoothly mixed.

Pour on top of chicken & cover up.

Store inside the refrigerator and let the chicken marinate overnight.

When ready to grill, do so over hot coals turning once until done.

Finish by garnishing with lime slices and cilantro.

Garlic Chicken

4 Boneless Skinless Chicken Breast Halves
1 Tablespoon of Lime Juice
1 Cup of Picante Sauce
2 Garlic Cloves, Minced
2 Tablespoons of Vegetable Oil
1/2 of Teaspoon Dried Oregano
1/2 Teaspoon of Ground Cumin
1/4 Teaspoon of Salt

Place each chicken breast in between 2 pieces of plastic cling wrap.

Using a meat mallet flatten the chicken to a 1/4-inch in thickness and then cut into 1-inch pieces.

Place everything in a shallow container.

Combine next 7 ingredients and mix well.

Pour everything over chicken and cover.

Chill for 1-2 hours.

Thread chicken on to skewers and cook over hot coals for 6-8 minutes or until done, turning occasionally and basting with remaining marinade as needed.

Serve with additional picante sauce.

Chicken Marinade

6 Boneless Skinless Chicken Breast Halves
1/4 Cup of Cider Vinegar
1 Lime, Juiced
1/2 Lemon, Juiced
1/2 Cup of Brown Sugar
3 Garlic Cloves, Peeled & Minced
1-1/2 Teaspoons of Salt
Ground Black Pepper to Taste
6 Tablespoons of Olive Oil
3 Tablespoons of Prepared Coarse-Ground Mustard

Mix together your cider vinegar, garlic, whole grain mustard, brown sugar, lime juice, lemon juice, & salt into a medium sized bowl.

Next, add olive oil & pepper.

Whisk together the mixture & place your chicken inside the mixture.

Cover & let the chicken marinate in the refrigerator overnight, or at least up to 8 hours.

Preheat your outdoor grill. Have it set on high & lightly oil the grate.

Place the marinated chicken on the grill, and cook each side for 10 minutes. Make sure the chicken is no longer pink inside and that the juices run clear.

You can throw out any marinade you may have remaining.

Grill Masters

BEEF

Beef Sauces

What says barbecue better than beef?

The **grill masters** have brought their very best insider recipes used in national cook off events and we've even included a fun kabob recipe just to make things interesting.

Barbecued Chuck Roast

4 Pounds of Round (7-Bone Chuck Roast), Cut 2"
thick
2 Teaspoons of Meat Tenderizer
3 Green Onions, Chopped
1 Garlic Clove
1/4 of a Green Pepper, Diced
2 Stalks of Celery, Diced
1/2 Teaspoon of Oregano
1/2 Teaspoon of Rosemary
1 Dash of Cayenne
1 Tablespoon of Worcestershire Sauce
3/4 Cup of Burgundy Wine
3 Tablespoons of Peanut Oil

Begin by cutting off the fat around the edges.

Sprinkle both sides of your roast with meat tenderizer
until it is evenly coated.

Using a fork, make deep piece marks all over the
meat, the place the meat in shallow dish.

Top the roast with green onions, green pepper, garlic,
celery, cayenne, oregano, and rosemary.

Next combine your Worcestershire sauce with the
burgundy wine and peanut oil. Once you are finished,
pour the mixture over top of the meat.

Let the meat sit in the refrigerator overnight. You will
need to turn meat several times and spoon the
chopped ingredients so they sit back on top.

Once that is done, sear both sides of the roast over top the glowing coals.

Raise the grill and continue cooking. You will want to have the meat about six inches from heat source.

50 to 60 minutes is the recommended time allowed for a complete and through grilling.

Using any leftover marinade, it is recommended you brush the roast frequently while grilling.

Bourbon Steak

1 - 1/2 Pounds of Steak
1 Teaspoon of Sugar
2 Tablespoons of Water
1 Garlic Clove, Crushed
1/4 Cup of Bourbon
2 Tablespoons of Soy Sauce

This simple recipe works well with any cut of steak.

Mix all listed ingredients together inside zip lock bag &
marinate the steak overnight, or at least 4 hours

Ready your grill for a hot fire.

Grill the steak to your desired perfection.

Tangy Rib Eye Steaks

4 (10 ounces) of Beef Rib Eye Steaks
1/2 Cup of Soy Sauce
1/2 Teaspoon of Sesame Oil
1/4 Teaspoon of Tabasco Sauce
1/2 Cup of Beer
1/4 Cup of Real Maple Syrup
6 Garlic Cloves, Minced
1 Tablespoon of Grated Fresh Ginger
1 Teaspoon of Mustard Powder

Blend the soy sauce, maple syrup, chopped garlic, grated ginger root, sesame oil, & Tabasco sauce inside a medium size mixing bowl.

Once thoroughly mixed, add the beer & gently stir.

Begin setting up the steaks by cutting any fat from the outsides of the steak.

Set your steaks in a new bowl & pour the marinade over top.

Take a fork & begin punching holes in the meat. Doing so will achieve that the marinade properly penetrates steaks.

Turn over the steaks repeat the previous step.

Once finished, secure the meat in tin foil or cling wrap & let it marinate for an hour or more inside the refrigerator. Overnight marination is also allowed.

When ready to grill, preheat the barbecue to high heat.

Set your marinated steaks onto the grill and let one side sear for 15 seconds.

Next, turn over the steaks & let cook for about 5 minutes.

The achieve medium-rare quality, turn over again & cook for another 5 minutes, depending on how thick the meat is.

Marinated Steak Kabobs

1 Pound of Sirloin Steak, Cut in 2" Cubes
1 Cup of Onions, Chopped
1/2 Cup of Vegetable Oil
1 Tablespoon of Worcestershire Sauce
1 Teaspoon of Mustard, Prepared
1/2 Cup of Lemon Juice
1/4 Cup of Soy Sauce
2 Medium Sized Tomatoes, Quartered
1 Large Green Pepper, Cut Into 1" Pieces
2 Medium Sized Onions, Quartered

Start by sauteing the onion in oil then remove from the heat.

Stir in some lemon juice, add a dash of soy sauce, Worcestershire, & some mustard then pour over the meat & vegetables.

Cover everything up & marinate overnight in your refrigerator.

Remove the meat & vegetables from marinade but do not throw out the marinade.

Alternate placing the meat cubes & vegetables on skewers.

Prepare the coals/grill & cook the kabobs for 5 minutes on each side while frequently brushing on the marinade.

Grill Masters

PORK

Pork Rubs

Beef isn't the only game in town when it comes to steaks. The grill masters' pork steak topped off with their secret rub will have your next cookout raving and coming back for more.

Grilled Pork Shoulder Steaks

8 Boneless Pork Shoulder Steaks, Cut 3/4-Inch Thick
1-1/2 Tablespoons of Hungarian Paprika
1 Tablespoon of Ground Coriander
1 Teaspoon of Salt
2 Teaspoons of Garlic Powder
1/4 Teaspoon of Caraway Seeds, Crushed
3/4 Teaspoon of Freshly Ground Black Pepper
1/2 Teaspoon of Ground Cumin
1/4 Teaspoon of Ground Cinnamon
1 Tablespoon of Lemon Zest, Finely Grated
1 Tablespoon of Dried Marjoram

Combine lemon zest, marjoram, cumin, paprika, coriander, caraway seeds, garlic powder, salt, pepper, & cinnamon into a small bowl

Firmly press & rub the herb mixture on to both sides of the steak.

Set the steaks in the middle of your grill.

Grill for 12 to 14 minutes at about 170F to achieve well-done perfection. Turn the steaks once over halfway through grilling time (6-7 minutes).

Grill Masters

FISH

GRILLED FISH

Health conscious barbecue lovers have lots of options
when it comes to cooking out as well.
The **Grill Masters** of their oriental halibut.

If you're searching something exotic, tasty and
packed with healthy benefits - look no further.

Grilled Halibut with Oriental Sauce

4 6-oz. Halibut Steaks, Cleaned
1/4 Cup of Orange Juice
1/2 Teaspoon of Pepper
2 Tablespoons of Fresh Parsley
2 Tablespoons of Soy Sauce
2 Tablespoons of Ketchup
2 Tablespoons of Vegetable Oil
1 Tablespoon of Fresh Lemon Juice
1/2 Teaspoon of Oregano
1 Garlic Clove, Minced

Mix together your soy sauce, ketchup, oil, pepper, garlic, parsley, orange juice, lemon juice, & oregano into a bowl.

Evenly brush the mixture on to the all the steaks, then refrigerate.

Once ready to cook, brush the grill lightly with oil.

Light the coals or gas grill to achieve a medium fire.

Set the steaks on the rack and begin cooking.

Give each side about 5 to 6 minutes, only turning once.

Grill Masters

RIBS

Ribs Sauce

When you think barbecue no doubt the picture a giant rack of ribs slathered in sauce with a side of fries and coleslaw.

The **grill masters** have assembled their top four award-winning rib recipes in this collection for your enjoyment.

Memphis-Style Barbecued Ribs

3 Pound Racks of Baby Back Ribs
2 Teaspoons of Salt
2 Teaspoons of Black Pepper, Coarse Ground
1 Cup of Red Wine Vinegar
1 Teaspoon of Louisiana Hot Sauce
2 Cups of Ketchup
2 Lemons, Thinly Sliced
2 Cups of Onions, Chopped
2 Garlic Cloves, Minced
1/4 Cup of Mustard, Yellow Prepared
1/2 Cup of Brown Sugar, Packed
Apple Juice for Basting

Prepare by trimming the fat from the ribs.

Loosen the membrane so as to get a firm enough grip, then peel it off the rack.

With a paring knife, scrape remaining fat from the bone.

Sprinkle the ribs on both sides with light coat of both salt & pepper.

Place the ribs, bone-side-down onto the grill.

Cook over a low fire for 1 1/2 hours, turning over the ribs every 15 to 20 minutes. Replenish the fire as necessary.

Baste the meat with apple juice at every turn. Do this only during first half of cooking the period. You can do this by either brushing on or using spray bottle.

Combine the mustard, sugar, vinegar, hot sauce, onion, & garlic in a blender & blend until smooth.

Place into a saucepan and add the ketchup. Let it simmer for 20 minutes.

Add the slices of lemon next.

Occasionally stir to keep it from sticking. Use the sauce as a frequent baste for the last half of the cooking period. Whether grilling or smoking, being careful not to burn the ribs.

Serve with the remaining sauce on the side.

Baby Back Ribs With Mustard Sauce

4 Pounds of Pork Spareribs
1/3 Cup of Brown Sugar
1/4 Cup of Vinegar
1/2 Teaspoon of Celery Seed
1/4 Cup of Onion, Finely Chopped
1/4 Cup of Mustard
1/4 Teaspoon of Garlic Powder

To make the sauce, take a saucepan and combine the vinegar, mustard, garlic powder, onion, celery seed, & brown sugar.

Bring it to boiling, while stirring, until till sugar dissolves.

Next, preheat grill & adjust the heat for indirect cooking.

Place your ribs on the rack over a medium heat.

Cover and grill for 1 1/4 to 1 1/2 hours. You want the ribs to be tender with no remaining pink.

Brush occasionally with the sauce during the last 15 minutes of grilling time.

Oven BBQ Ribs

3 Pounds of Pork Back Ribs
8 Ounces of Jar Honey
1/4 Cup of White Sugar
1/4 Teaspoon of Fresh Ground Pepper
1 Teaspoon of Paprika
12 Ounces of Barbecue Sauce
1 Medium Sized Onion, Finely Chopped
1 Teaspoon of Chili Powder
1/2 Teaspoon of Onion Powder
1/4 Teaspoon of Celery Salt
1/2 Cup of Dark Brown Sugar
2 Tablespoons of Old Bay Seasoning
1/2 Teaspoon of Garlic Powder

Add all ingredients together into a big roasting pan.

Slice the ribs apart for easier serving.

Combine together while making sure to apply coating to all the ribs with this semi-dry spread.

Disperse the ribs out evenly on to the bottom of the pan & lightly cover with tin foil.

Bake at 375F for about 1 hour while turning & stirring occasionally.

Pineapple Baby Back Ribs

1 -2 Pounds of Slab Baby Back Pork Ribs
3 Cups of Pineapple Juice
1/3 Cup of Ketchup
2 Teaspoons of Ground Ginger
4 Garlic Cloves, Minced
1/3 Cup of Red Wine Vinegar
1/2 Teaspoon of Cayenne Pepper
1-1/2 Tablespoons of Fresh Lemon Juice
2 Tablespoons of Soy Sauce
1/2 Teaspoon of Ground Cloves
1-1/2 Cups of Brown Sugar
1-1/2 Tablespoons of Mustard Powder
12 Ounces of Bottled Barbecue Sauce

In a glass bowl, mix the brown sugar, mustard powder, red wine vinegar, ketchup, lemon juice, pineapple juice, & soy sauce together.

Next add the ginger, cayenne pepper, cloves, & garlic.

Slice the ribs into pieces & then set them into the marinade.

Cover and place inside the refrigerator. Remember to turn occasionally & let marinate overnight or at least a minimum of 8 hours.

Preheat your oven to 275F. & place the marinated ribs into a baking dish. Cover with marinade while letting it cook for 1 1/2 hours, turning every once in a while to ensure it cooks evenly.

If you are grilling outdoors, preheat your grill to medium heat.

Let the ribs cook on the grill for about 15 to 20 minutes while turning often. Use barbecue sauce to baste with.

Ribs Rubs

It's all about the rub. Barbecue just isn't barbecue without proper preparation.

We've given you the standard Kansas City style rub along with something unique – an Apple smoked rub featuring cinnamon for a unique sweet taste you're sure to return to again and again.

Apple Smoked Barbecue Ribs

2 Slabs of Baby Back Ribs
1/2 Teaspoon of Cinnamon
1 Cup of Apple Wood Chips
1/2 Teaspoon of Ground Cloves
1/4 Teaspoon of Pepper
Barbecue Sauce (Recipe Follows)

Preheat the oven to 400F.

Rub the cinnamon, cloves, & pepper onto both sides of the ribs.

Set the ribs on a wire rack on a baking pan.

Bake for 3 hours until the ribs become tender.

Soak the wood chips in water for 30 minutes & prepare the grill.

Place the apple wood chips in the center the coals.

Baste the ribs & set them on the grill just above wood chips.

Cover & cook for 10 minutes.

Then turn over the ribs, baste again, & continue cooking for another 10 minutes (or at least until the ribs are brown & moist)

Barbecue Sauce:
2-15 oz. cans of tomato sauce
1/2 cup of red wine vinegar

10 cloves of garlic
1/2 cup of molasses
2 tablespoons of dry mustard
Freshly ground pepper
1/4 teaspoon of hot pepper flakes
2 tablespoons of ground cumin
1/2 teaspoon of cinnamon

Add all ingredients (except vinegar) into a pan.
Simmer, with the lid on, on low heat for 1 hour, while
occasionally stirring.

Add vinegar to taste & simmer for 15 more minutes.

Chill until ready to use.

Kansas City Rib Rub

1 Tablespoon of Salt
1/2 Cup of Brown Sugar
1/4 Cup of Paprika
1 Tablespoon of Chili Powder
1 Teaspoon of Cayenne
1 Tablespoon of Black Pepper
3/4 Tablespoon of Onion Powder
3/4 Tablespoon of Garlic Powder

Combine all listed ingredients together & store inside an air tight food container or bag.

Grill Masters WINGS

Wings Sauce

Its game time and all the fans are assembled around the TV.

Why not treat them to something memorable? Serve them the *grill masters* honey cinnamon wings and they may just forget all about the game!

Cinnamon Honey Wings

2-1/2 Pounds of Chicken Wings
4 Garlic Cloves, Chopped
1/4 Cup of Olive Oil
2 Tablespoons of Soy Sauce
1/4 Cup of Vinegar, Rice
1/4 Cup of Honey, Mild
1-1/2 Teaspoons of Cinnamon, Ground
1 Teaspoon of Thyme
1/2 Teaspoon of Ginger, Ground
1/2 Teaspoon of Mustard, Dry

Mix all listed ingredients inside a plastic bag, then knead periodically for 2 hours.

Prepare a fire in grill.

Cook the wings on the grill for approximately 10 minutes on one side, turn & baste with the marinade.

Continue grilling for an additional 10 minutes on the other side, or until fully cooked.

Grill Masters SHRIMP

Shrimp Sauce

Shrimp with barbecue sauce is a great summer time treat. It's easy to make and it's easy to scale up for any size crowd.

The **Grill masters** shrimp on the Barbie special sauce will treat your guests to a feast that would do Crocodile Dundee proud!

Shrimp on The Barbie

12 Giant Prawns, Shelled
1/4 Cup of Butter
2 Green Onions, Tops & White
1 Teaspoon of Ginger Root, (Freshly Grated)
2 Tablespoons of Sherry
1 Teaspoon of Orange Zest (grated)
1 Cup of Orange Juice (Freshly, Squeezed)

Let 12 wooden skewers soak in water for 30 minutes.

Add 1 prawn to each skewer from head to tail.

Mix all listed ingredients (except for the prawns) into a pan & cook on medium/low heat. Stir periodically until the butter is fully melted.

Dip the skewered prawns into the sauce & then place them on the grill about 4 inches above the coals.

Use the sauce to heavily baste & grill for 2 minutes.

Turn over the prawns & continue to baste again while cooking for 2 more minutes.

Smaller prawn will be cooked after about 4 minutes of grilling, but for larger prawn, repeat the process of turning & basting until your prawns are pink or thoroughly cooked to your liking.

Once finished grilling, quickly remove the prawns from the heat source to prevent them from getting too tough.

Use any leftover sauce as a dip if you so choose.

GrillMasters

MISC

Misc. Sauces

Barbecue is loved the world over and it's one of the fastest-growing segments around. We didn't want to leave anything out some assembled a little bit of everything in this last section including some beer and whiskey infused concoctions for those of you who want to try something with a real kick!

Beer Barbecue Sauce

1 Cup of Prepared Barbecue Sauce
1 Cup of Ketchup
2 Tablespoons of Dijon Mustard
1/4 Cup of Honey or Molasses
2 Tablespoons of Lemon Juice
1 Tablespoon of Worcestershire Sauce
2 Garlic Cloves, Minced
2/3 Cup of Beer
2 Tablespoons of Red Wine Vinegar
1 Teaspoon of Hot Pepper Sauce
1/2 Teaspoon of Pepper
2 Onions, Finely Chopped

Take a big bowl & start by mixing the beer, mustard honey, hot pepper sauce, garlic, pepper, lemon juice, barbecue sauce, onions, ketchup, vinegar, & Worcestershire sauce.

Add the food of your choice into the marinade & let it sit at room temperature for about 2 hours, or in the refrigerator overnight.

Once prepared to grill, remove the food & put the marinade in a saucepan.

Cook for about 10 minutes or until it becomes thickened.

Use it as sauce for basting or being served with cooked food.

Honey Spiced BBQ Sauce

1-1/4 Cup of Catchup
1 Cup of Honey
2 Tablespoons of Dry Mustard
3 Teaspoons of Ginger, Fresh Grated
2/3 Cup of Salad Oil
1 Lemon, Sliced Thinly
3 Tablespoons of Butter
3/4 Cup of Vinegar
5 Tablespoons of Worcestershire Sauce

Mix all listed ingredients into a pan & heat them up until they blend together.

Take out the lemon peels before basting.

Jack Daniel's Grilling Sauce

1/4 Cup of Jack Daniel's Whiskey
1/2 Cup of Pineapple Juice
1-1/2 Teaspoon Garlic Powder
3 Tablespoons Soy Sauce

Mix all listed ingredients together into a bowl and stir.

Dip the meat into the sauce & place it over hot coals.

Brush with sauce before turning the meat over.

Continue grilling until satisfaction.

Just before you remove the meat from the grill, brush it again with the sauce.

Watermelon Barbecue Sauce

1-6 Pound Chunk of Seedless Watermelon
1 Tablespoon of Garlic Powder
1/2 Cup of Sherry
2 Teaspoons of Lemon juice
2 Cups of Firmly Packed Brown Sugar
1 Teaspoon of Liquid Smoke
8 Ounces of Tomato Paste
1 Tablespoon of Onion Powder

Slice the watermelon into chunks & dump them into a saucepan.

Let them cook uncovered on medium heat until they turn to the consistency of applesauce. (This will take about 2–3 hours).

Stir occasionally.

Mix in the remaining listed ingredients.

Allow the mixture to simmer on low heat for 2 more hours.

Once the time is up, let it cool back to room temperature before applying to food.

Tennessee BBQ Sauce

1 Cup of Catchup
1 Onion, Chopped
1/2 Cup of Brown Sugar
2 Cups of Water
1/2 Cup of Vinegar
1/4 Cup of Worcestershire Sauce
1/2 Teaspoon of Salt
1 Teaspoon of Celery Seed

Mix all ingredients into a small pan and heat it until boiling.

Let it simmer until it becomes a thick sauce while stirring periodically.

Molasses Orange Barbecue Sauce

1 Can of Condensed Tomato Soup (10-3/4 Ounces)
1 Can of Tomato Sauce, (8 Ounces)
1/2 Cup of Molasses, Light
1/2 Cup of Vinegar
1/2 Cup of Brown Sugar, Packed
1/4 Cup of Vegetable Oil
1 Tablespoon of Minced Onion, Instant
1 Tablespoon of Seasoned Salt
1 Tablespoon of Dry Mustard
1 Tablespoon of Worcestershire Sauce
1 Tablespoon of Orange Peel, Finely Shredded
1-1/2 of Teaspoon Paprika
1/2 of Teaspoon Pepper, Black
1/4 of Teaspoon Garlic Powder

Take a pan & mix all listed ingredients.

Heat the mixture until boiling, then reduce heat & let it simmer for about 20 minutes.

Carolina BBQ Rub

2 Tablespoons of Salt
2 Tablespoons of Black Pepper, Freshly Ground
1 Tablespoon of Cayenne Pepper
1/4 Cup of Paprika
2 Tablespoons of Sugar
2 Tablespoons of Brown Sugar
2 Tablespoons of Ground Cumin
2 Tablespoons of Chili Powder

Mix all listed ingredients into a small bowl and mix thoroughly.

This can be used as a dry rub for beef, lamb, chicken, or pork.

Cajun Blackening Spices

5 Teaspoons of Paprika
1 Teaspoon of Cayenne Pepper
1/2 Teaspoon of Garlic Powder
1/2 Teaspoon of Black Pepper, Finely Ground
1/2 Teaspoon of White Pepper, Finely Ground
1 Teaspoon of Ground Oregano, Dried
1 Teaspoon of Ground Thyme, Dried

Combine and store together inside an air-tight
container or bag.

Don't Miss The Companion Edition to this Book!

http://bit.do/bbq2

Check out other titles from us @

2ndEmpireMedia.Com

Printed in Great Britain
by Amazon